From the library of

_____

Rhymes of a Woodman's Path

By Jacob Burnard

PUBLISHED BY BURNIE BOOKS
26100 NEWPORT ROAD STE 12-114
MENIFEE, CA 92584

www.facebook.com/burniebooks

COPYRIGHT © 2016 BY JACOB BURNARD

ALL RIGHTS RESERVED

PRINTED IN THE UNITED STATES OF AMERICA

ISBN-10: 0692622128
ISBN-13: 978-0692622124

PREFACE

In recent and sometimes not so near dealings of life, dreams, and the rhythms of my mind battling and building itself, it seems necessary to begin writing rhymes, stories, a diary—poetry; moreover, it is essential: for if I desire to continue my life and my chosen journey in a sanely way my conscious mind requires this.

Up to now, and presumably into the future as I continue to break through the enigma of my subconscious mind, my thoughts, more times than not, are encoded in riddles and rhymes: rhymes let me hide myself in art and imagery and riddles prevent me from finding the truths my heart so desperately desires. I believe both constructs are products of my mind holding the keys to my soul.

I asked myself, what could possibly bring this on? Why write a book? Why share my thoughts with the world? The list is long and many reasons come to mind; one thing did impress me: a question my daughter suggested, "What if one of every animal in the universe is you and you just didn't know it? We could turn into an eagle and fly anywhere we want to go." What if? What if the only thing holding me back was my mind telling me I could not turn into an eagle, when, if I would only allow that to happen I could be soaring through the sky, and through the façade of my own precepting.

Through this writing experience I intend to expose fallacies within the many complexities of my mind and my heart and my soul, whereby I may look into a mirror and see the previous me, the present me, and the future me—together. Furthermore, dear reader, mayhap your complex trails converge with mine on this meandering river of existence.

DEDICATION

For my mother Victoria.

After she moved on from our world I found an old spiral notebook, which was once hers. The first few pages contained some writing: a shopping list for the grocery store, a budget for the month, and some miscellaneous notes. I ripped those pages out and threw them away. I thumbed through the rest of the blank pages of lined paper, and amongst them, in the middle of the notebook, these words were written on the middle of the page, in her hand, "we use our minds unconsciously. The key is to be conscious of the way we use our mind." I remember as though this happened yesterday: I was in the garage sitting on top of the washing machine, staring at a message my mother had somehow sent from heaven. I cried. I carefully tore out this precious message, folded it, and put it in a little wood box, to rest amongst other sigils. At the time I would not fully understand the depths of those two sentences, being nineteen. And, mayhap I never will. I love you Mom.

CONTENTS

Introduction   1
    Writing Lies of Truth

Prayers   3
    Prayer Priori   4
    Prayer of The Sea   5

Love Letters   7
    Venus and Jupiter   8
    Fear for Love of Lust   9
    Ballad of a Mountain Man   11
    Goddess of Men   14
    Fused   15
    Aemelia   17
    Clutch The Gypsy's Blood   18
    E Amor et Sapientia Venistas   19

Gun and Key	21
Butterfly	22
Mountain Spires	23
She's on the Trail	24
Atoms in Love	25
Rowena	26
Subtitles	27
Loved One Lost and Gone	28
Captivated	29
Love Pangs	30
The Eye of Death	31
Tall Maiden	33

Childish   35

Child in Darkness	36
Piano in The Stars	38

A girl Who's Only Three   40
   The Art of a Child   41

Grizzly   43

   Meeting Grizzly   44
   Dream better left unseen   46
   Palaver   47
   Battle   48

On The Trail   51

   Stone in Hand   52
   Blade Out of Stone   53
   Live Oak Tree   54
   Peckerwood   56
   Purity is a Dirty Word   58

Diary of a Madman	59
The River of Israel	71
The Highway	71
The House	79
The Town	89
The Bank	97
About The Author	134

Rhymes of a Woodman's Path

By Jacob Burnard

Some things like a tornado can be admired for its beauty, its sway, the way it spins and moves across the plains, and just as we revere the power of nature, we must do so, too, with regard to the power of man; for some men follow a conscious path, while others meander without a care. Both scenes relay beauty, and both scenes are here, but only one is aware of their art.

Introduction

Writing lies of truth

That growing flowing nature call
That sounds harmonic to us all:
We write! We fight! We cannot lie!
But we put the Devil in disguise.

Show our soul just a little bit
So we can go on living it.

That growing flowing murder call
That sounds demonic to us all:
We stab! We bleed! We lie to me!
And the Devil's eyes we come to meet.

Our souls shone out, the truth to see
The devil that resides in me.

That growing flowing loving call
That sounds angelic to us all:
We fight! We bleed! We write the three!
Our souls to walk the Earth and breathe.

Prayers

The prayers of a man are the gateway to his soul.

Prayer Priori

I am the transcendental one.
Through synergy I've found my reason to be.
Though not presumed to be magnificent,
I'm still vital to the lock—
The key: one of many.

It is my honor and my creed
To be considered one of these
In control of the current and the tide—
Floating in the sea.

Prayer of the Sea

This has been and never was.
It is and never will.

Helm of the fairing seas;
Dark grey gusts of Winters' needs
Draught through lines he hath not seen
Hast brought me here to be with me,
Eternally.

Eternally me which be to hear;
I show—have told it has not lines.
From across draught needs
Leads Winters' wind and dark grey seas;
Faring the helm of Will to be.

Never is it. And never was never
And stood has this—forever and ever.
Aye!

Love Letters

We will be together in a kiss, my Aemilia. A kiss more gentle that a butterfly's wings sweeping amaranthus petals through dreams of morning starlight; on lips that sparkle with the light of your eyes, I will be with you, trembling in the reverie of our love.

Venus and Jupiter

Watch the divine dance in each-other's light to-night.
See them walk close to one-another. See them shine.
See him plod slowly, waiting for the union of his lost love;
See her run wanting for the coming of her true love lost.

Watch them dance. Sing to their mortal beauty.
Sing the song of lovers lost and love to come.
Sing with lips that long to fill in the void of futility.
Sing, and feel the drums in your heart beat.

Watch the king without a queen sense her passing by.
Feel her dance and prance around the moonlit sky.
Feel the passion she holds for him burst into clouds.
Feel the rain drops dance in your eyes, feel her cries.

Watch the queen without a king get lost in his sight.
Hear his romance ring the bells of silent delight.
Hear the hailstrum rage from the bedrock through the Earth.
Hear the thunderbolts dance on your skin, feel him grin.

Watch the divine dance in each-other's light to-night.
You must see them—for they cannot see one-another.
You must feel them—for they are lost in one-another's light.
You must hear them—They have given all their love to us.

Tonight, sing to the one you love.
Don't let them pass you by.

Fear for Love of Lust

He woke up to see the valley view below, looked at the twisting wild river of mud and sand he has trekked behind and began to remember a time when he was a child-man: that very same river, however far gone in favor of memory, had swept him away and bayed he stay in a gyre four endless days—days of ecstasy and fear.

The ecstasy was of such intensity that love and lust were one in the same . . . so he thought: it was a constant rhythm of physical pleasure, without need for climax or end, reverberating within every cell, a lasting gratitude for the present.

The fear, I'm afraid to say, is much more difficult to describe: it was like the sensation of slowly suffocating by your own hands, as if you'd set a trap for some other creature; then, as you're falling, you've realized your going to die for your own fucking lack of memory—falling endlessly.

What manifest those days seemed to form from nothing at all, like a ghost, a doppelganger perhaps—a demon none the less. And so, he is dry as the match in his sealed tin can. He has always only been on the edge of either cut-bank or point-bar, but today is a new day, a different day that's sure; out of the westward corner of his left and right eye a shadow glides by. He sees a demon—his demon—laughing back at him.

Ballad of a Mountain Man

*The spin of her six shot
Turned my head toward her sights:
It's a gleaming and she's a glaring
Down that long colt 45.*

Her eyes, they have found you.
They've found their way into your soul,
And they leer with the brilliance
Of browns, greens, blues, and golds.

A beauty one can hardly compare
To the Rocky Mountains at autumn;
Where the trees change their leaves
And the scene takes you hostage.

They spiral and spin
through the air and the wind;
One hue moves through the next,
And each moment the colors, they come alive!

They spiral and spread, they edge and dredge
They creep even deeper and deeper;
And she fills you thoughts with beauty and dread;
Maybe she's an angle, but she might be a reaper.

Crawl under the carriage and get under that bearskin.
Be quiet and be still, she's still walking around.

She's whirlin' through the village. She's tearin' it apart.
It's you she wants, Will, and she won't stop lookin'

The town has become silent. Everything is still.
They're waiting for a fight, or the submission of his will.

Men with faded faces facing William's gaze
Stand like granite statues along the boardwalk pine.

While women wearing white satin dresses stay wanting,
looking through black iron curtains
From second story windows,
Waiting for another faded face.

But through the runnin' and the mumblin'
They failed to see his strategy.
And as she walked through his mind
She fell mercy to his grizzly.

The protector of his soul; the pardoner of his misery.
The bear stands guard to tear the heart from any enemy

Grizzly and me, we made a deal we could both win.
So we let her walk around, to see what or who she is.

And while he is lost in her stare and the colors and the care,
And the feel of her riding into his heart and his snare.

She is trapped in my thoughts. Yes, I too had a plan,
A contingency, if you will, of a solitary Mountain Man.

Two Souls wishing and waiting, wanting a special touch:
Searching in a deserted war for a battle worthy of love.

Goddess of Men

You cannot stage a place in your mind
That she cannot freely flee:

How dare you view her in your stupor
As a place to justly dump your seed!

She is disgusted in your thoughts and of your wants
Of what you think to deem her be.

You cannot touch her!
You cannot defile an ideal!

She is a real maiden
She is inspiration

She is Calliope,
And she is Thalia

She is a shooting star dancing
through a river of endless wonder

Looking to those
Who truly love her.

Fused

My dreams revive my ideas
Brought by elusive thoughts and wants:
The future of our life, of her and I
Visions in waves and haunts;

Nights in an alternate life
Where her and I are mutually sought,
Enraptured by the highest contract
Brought by the bond of a mystic wand;

Abscond to night through desperate light
In sights before the sun,
Where apprehension fills the air
With musk and piercing bugs

We are flooded under a restless canopy
Where leaves drop through goliath trees,

And now our star has faded away,
Further into new unseen places:
Ipomoea alba noctiflora braves the nave
And takes the place left by silent larks.

Embracing
Taking her through rays of rainbow clouds

Doused in fallen petals of ruffled feathers

Aroused
from flight, housed in the skylight of muse

Fused
Forever falling, calling, down to the ground.

Aemilia

Let us live, my Aemilia, let us love

And of all the gods and goddesses of old
With all their stories told
Are grains of sand to us

And once our love has transformed this place
Let us explore, and explode
Into new beautiful universes

And once we have made enough new worlds
Let us travel beyond space
Where time does not exist

And while we are there, let us stare
Into the oceans of our love
And become entranced

And when we have gazed long enough to forget
Let us become humans once more,
So I can find you, again, and say

Let us live, My Aemilia, let us love
For all eternity.

Clutch the Gypsy's Blood

She's the one who clutches
Hold the gypsy man's blood

I will show you love and give you lust.
My splendor will enmesh and test you.

Leave your dreams and follow me
And I will fulfill your life with all I need.

So long as you surrender to only me
Existence will seem as though you're free

The cosmos dare not catch your eye
Or I will stab you and bleed you dry;

Take the energy that is meant for you
And use it for things I feel to do.

She is the one who harbors
Inside the invalid soul.

E Amor et Sapientia Venistas

Aurora intra ante amor dico vale sapientia.
Within the dawn before love I say farewell to wisdom.

Love before wisdom and wisdom before love.
Are these not virtues? One begets the other;
They were born in the same moment.

Ancient man, and some not so old,
Loves the land and the wind and the moon
For he can see the life she gives
Loves his woman and her eyes
For he can see the live she gives

You may argue that ancient men were not this way
And I'll say, today, not all men are contrary.

Man is the sun and the air and the fire;
Man holds the cup of love
I know, once, this was so.

Ancient woman, and some not so old,
Loves the fire and the air and the sun
For she can see the life he gives
Loves her man and his eyes
For she can see the life he gives

You may argue that ancient women were not this way
And I'll say, today, not all women are contrary.

Woman is the moon and the wind and the land;
Woman holds the cup of wisdom
I know, once, this was so.

Man before woman or woman before man
Are these not virtues? One begets the other;
They were born in the same moment.

Within love and wisdom,
I say hello to the dawn of beauty.

Gun and Key

Long ago a king pulled a gun
From a fire burning in the sky
To share with his queen
For all eternity.

The queen soon came
With a gift of her own
She had pulled from
A hole in the night.

As their gifts became one
Their thoughts became many
Scattered through space and time.

In the moment they touched,
Into fragments of glass and sand
They became.

And the gun fell to Earth still longing
For love to pull the trigger, again.

Butterfly

I am lost in thoughts of you, my love;
Like a memory of another night
Waning on waxing moonlight,
Under shadows of cloud cover.

Oh Moon! Why do you wane so?
Yesterday your glow was full
And today you came to me
On fluttering butterfly wings.

Oh Moon! You are always whole in the sky.
Only, sometimes your light hides
From the trails of my mind.
My heart is yours and yours is mine.

Mountain Spires

A bolt of shadowed light
From out this mountain shining, blinding,
My eyes are searching for you,
Over an endless pit I stand.

A bare breasted beauty
From out this window running, jumping,
She brushes her fingers on my chest,
Into the abyss she slowly falls.

A bare beautiful mind
From out this door dreaming, leaping,
She looks at me to save her,
Into the abyss she wails and screams.

A bare bolt of light
From out this mountain rolling springing,
She wraps her legs around my me,
Into eternal love we fall.

A thunder through us echoes
From in our lightning striking, rising,
We move the world around us,
Time holds eternity's breath.

She is on the Trail

Love is the gift fused through the beauty
Of human souls and divine love.

She reads these cedar tree carvings
Etched with the power of past romances.

She smells dark red velvet roses
Flowing from the daydreams of your kisses.

She tastes sweet amaranthus honey
Swirling through her tongue.

She feels the firmness of your finger
Gently gliding across her lips.

She hears you singing with the wind
from every sun shining mountain peak.

She is on the trail walking with the trees
Tangled up in your loving embrace.

Atoms in Love

Do atoms know how thoughtless they are?
Selfish of them to be in love,
The way they push and pull on one another;
Selfish to become one.

Do planets know how foolish they are?
Selfish of them to be in love,
The way they push and pull on one another;
Selfish to become one.

Do people know how silly they are?
Selfish of them to be in love,
The way they push and pull on one another;
Selfish to become one.

What might the world be like if love did not exist?

Rowena

Her eyes were part hazel and part light blue,
Depending on how dilated the pupils
That centered the scene had been.

The farthest extent from the light blue of her eyes
Were lassoed by a color similar to the midnight sky,
Where a dark moon gently peaked over hills in the distance.

It's hard to explain the look she gave at the end of those long nights,
She liked the way I touched her . . . So gentle and kind,
As though I expected nothing in return.

That was when she would look me at with those eyes
And her smile that went off to one side;
Her passion lured me in.

Subtitles

You are the greatest riddle in my life,
Like Pandora's Box you are locked away
Within the worlds of my heart and brain.

Your great escape is through a maze
Weaved with rhythmic subtitles and rhymes:
Phantasmal assailants of my crimes.

My punishment, it seems to be,
Is living only half my life in imaginary write:
Where you can see the soul in me.

But you will not get the whole of me.

Loved One Lost and Gone

There is something strange to say
For loved ones gone to the grave:
Their body and soul don't solely go,
They take a whole lot more.

A piece ripped away with the waves;
Their memories sit on distant shores.

My memories of her and I
Are strangled by fate and time.
Unless I make a catchy rhyme;
Make a greater imprint on my mind.

Although, these memories are far lost and gone;
And still I choose to write and rhyme with you
In a land free to believe in make-believe.

Captivated

Just another day at the coffee shop
Seeing the people and drinkin' my usual brew;
When unexpectedly a change, a lady, a natural beauty,
A beauty only scribed by literary rhyme.

She's a foot away and there is nothing I can say
Through the coffee shop talkin' and noise.
All I can do is write about the beautiful view,
And make signs more settle than a mime.

Bold. No sugar or cream. Just a hint of ice to calm.
I can't wait long for the moment of my first sip.
Captivated and lost, willing to risk it all;
Stuck in the shape of her lips.

Though I've got to go, she must know
The sensations she has caused in my soul;
She has ellipsed my heart with her physical art
I can no longer hold my self control!

I don't know what to say, *Hi, my name is Jake.*
Today you've taken away my breath.
She looks at me and squints her eye
And shyly says, *Elizabeth.*

Love Pangs

Surly my love for you is evolving;
Around every corner I can see the story
Unfold in a blink of an eye.

I see our love in scenes of times past,
Of futures unfolding,
And dimensions at rest.

What a beautiful tragedy: to see everything
From the outside looking in.
Surly, this is the plight of the gods!

The Eye of Death

The hour of the sun shines for his dove,
And the hour of the moon for her love.

A man does not fear death,
And a dove does not fear the hawk by her side,
Their eyes never cease to meet; their hearts are one.

A man walks into the face of death,
And looks him straight in the eye many times,
They stand resolute; until the day they embrace
Man's love stands with you.

And from the sky a phantom's feather falls
Spiraling toward the ground with a sound saying,
Good job old chap, I will fly from you today;
Today you must remain a man.

Each flower he finds by a fluttering feather
He knows will show him the path to take
And with great strength he breathes
In the flower's scent and says:

I will fight and I will find you!
I will look Death in the eye!
I am the dove!
I am the hawk!
I am Death!

I will kill any beast that stands in my path!
Even still, if that beast be part of me
I will cut it out and let it bleed!

Anyone who dares to challenge my love
Will run like a dewdrop swallowed by the rising sun!
Like rodents will running with blood under the red moon!

And through these many battles, my love,
I will thank them, for bringing me this far,
For bringing me closer to you.

My love ultra aeviternitas

Tall maiden

I dreamt of you last night, my Aemilia.
You found your way through a tall maiden's laughter,
And as you lay by my side,
I swam with the aisles of your blue eyes—
Watching us see our love.
A cosmic force alive within two.
Spirits divine.
Alive on the rhythm of each wave,
With every small kiss,
with the brush of our fingertips,
whispering breezes through your hair—
She turns into butterflies.
Universes will move as our love collide.

Childish Letters

It is through a child's play the truth to heaven is paved.

Child In Darkness

She is shining in the midnight sky
Behind a horizon of moonlit hills:
Hazel, green, and grey, blue and brown,
Lassoed with bliss in black-blue brightness.

Beyond the boundless mountains of pines
The Moon rose slowly in the shade.
And as I peered through the needles in the night
I saw a child shinning in a sea of darkness.

She is skipping on the dark side of the moon,
Like a pupil within a ball of eclipsed walls;
Blindly full of joy and leaping across nothingness,
While she's rising through the sky's speckled halls.

I had to reach her! I screamed, "see me! I am here!"
But she did not hear me from her dark dreary sphere.
I ran to the mountains. I crawled through its fissures
Leading toward the oldest tree on its highest peak.

But the moon carried the little girl further away;
And I remained atop a cedar tree, praying.
I watched her travel the sky through the night.
I saw her pass Jupiter and Orion as she descended.

A dreadful feeling overcame me as she drew closer to the sea . . .
Fear washed through my spine like a rolling wave, trapped,
Spinning and churning in my chest with no way free.
I wished to pull her away from her burning darkness.

The door for the solar hoard began to open over the waters.
And as the sun began to peak through the trees
The sea began to glisten with the prism's ghosts,
Spreading their colors through the moon and me.

While the moon brought the little girl into the sea,
I watch her skipping and singing through a field
fragrant with flowers of every hue, formed from the sun—
All along it was only me who could not see.

Piano in The Stars

Who's in that picture on the wall Daddy?
Is that your friend? Asked a girl who's only three.
That's Daddy's Mommy, I replied.
How do I explain that she died to a girl who's only three?

My Mommy is up in heaven, she is up in the stars.
And although you've never met her and you've never seen her,
She isn't really that far:
A big part of my Mommy lives on, extremely strong, inside of me.

A few days later my little girl Kate had something to say:
In a somber voice she said to me, Daddy, I died the other day,
I died and went up in the sky, I went up to the stars,
And I saw your Mommy.

Your Mommy was in the stars and she was playing the piano.
And I came back!

In wonder I asked her what happened next.
She looked over at me from the corner of her eye,
And with a slight little sigh, she said, *nothing*.

Now, Kate is a great story teller;
She spins tales of bears and snakes and trees.
But for her to end a story so abruptly . . .
I know, this scene wasn't something she was preforming.

Nothing I say, nor anything I sing
Can illustrate the way Kate made me feel.
How could she have known about the piano?
The melody my Mother loved to hear.

A vision I've gained is forever engraved
And it came by way of my Daughter's dream;
Through her revelation or incarnation
She gave me a whole new image to see.

A Girl Who's only Three

She screams and shouts, *Daddy! Daddy! Daddy!*
She yells and belts, *Mommy! Mommy! Mommy!*
Don't go. Don't leave. She loves us both.
She wants you and me.

She's only three and she doesn't understand,
This is the way things have to be.

These transitions of love aren't awfully easy,
For a girl who's only three.

She wants us both. And this goes to show
That love just isn't free

There's pain in the girl that means everything
To a loving man, as me.

What can I do? This is something new,
To a Girl who's only three.

She'll be okay. She'll make out fine.
But there's something that hurts inside.
She yells and belts, *Mommy! Mommy! Mommy!*
She screams and shouts, *Daddy! Daddy! Daddy!*

The Art of a Child

There are so many thoughts, trepidatious props,
Locked in the mind of a child.

She's a girl of four and it's difficult to ignore,
The constructs that life beguiles

What's in that little girl mind
I cannot seem to find . . .
Dreams of gargoyles and dark?

Or a structure more real that seems too unclear
To cure her extrinsic charms?

So precious and pure . . . yet clouded with quiet.
Imagine . . . her path has already fashioned.

How could it be? She was only three . . .
And now . . . she sees illusions of her own

I would, if I only could, protect her from her heart!
Daddy, you've known since I was born . . .
You can't control the way I learn my art.

Grizzly

The angels who speak to us are many.
Their voice is calm; their voice is strong.

Meeting Grizzly

Grizzly, he's with me today
And grows even stronger with each passing phase
He's a gift I've gained; but where did he com from?
When exactly did I change?

You haven't changed a bit.
I've always been here. And I've always been inside.
But you kept me pushed down, kept me hidden,
And denied me as your guide.

There were a couple of times you needed my help,
I tried and I strained to escape;
And I met you in your dreams on a trail through the trees
To show you that I was here.

The second time I came closer, I almost made it through;
But my claws, they would only scrape.
Look at the scars on your arm, they were from me,
You must believe—I only wanted to help.

But you kept me locked away;
In fear—afraid I'd hurt the ones you'd loved.
And to tell you the truth, I would 'a been ruthless.
I'd 'a knocked out every last one!

I have just one more thing to say before you put me away,
Listen very close.
I'm ready to fight! I'm ready to do what's right!
For you and for those you've chose!

But if they don't love you back . . .
I'll attack and tear out their lying throats!
I'll expose who they really are!
I'll reveal all their secrets!

I'll render the truth from their soul.

Grizzly, I'm glad you are here, I have no reason to fear
The wrath from those of my foes

It's you and it's me, together we can be free
Together, we have repose.

Dream Better Left Unseen

Out of a slumber I rose to remember
A dream I had this night:
A dream of a day my daughter was taken away,
Taken out of my sight.

She was taken and murdered,
Killed with a knife and taken out of my life.
I couldn't control the thoughts in my head;
Illusions of revenge were rife.

They rifled through, they enthused my soul
And the depths of who I am . . . or what I'd become
If the little girl in the center of my world
Was hurled into the stars by scum

Grizzly and I discussed what we'd do . . .
We agreed that he would take the lead!
And together we would transmute into something new
We'd become a different kind of bread

And as we walked across the threshold,
The creed of the Grizzly branded our hide:
Help the innocent survive! Take no child slayer alive!
Grizzly will choose how you die.

Palaver With Grizzly

Grizzly and him sit above the mossy rock-rimmed brook
Under the early evening sky while slow moving sparks
Fly between the blue and brown of their eyes.

No, my dear friend, I'm not the end.
Repose is far from where you stand;
And I must confess . . .

The path ahead has many turns and several bends;
The trail is greater than the ground to set your feet,
It surrounds your mind

There are no blocked walls to guide you to the end;
No maze to take, only open doors for you to choose;
Past, present, and future.

I've a warning, I must say, there is something you lack.
Without this, you'll surely be raped, strangled, and snared . . .
Tortured by guilt and fear and disbelief;

Without a shield to wield to fight the shadows that demons be,
You will fall into walls of your own creating;
Please, recognize your creed!

Battle with Grizzly

Grizzly is growling and snarling at him;
For he forgot the line he once surrendered,
"For you and those you've chose . . ."
Now it's the truth in my soul he renders . . .

I've denied love of my life, Grizzly, I admit.
I was afraid of the pain.
How do I chose the perfect mate?

These questions you pose have no answers from me;
I have my part: I fight and frighten when I must;
And you have your part far above all of us . . .
You are the architect!

On The Trail

One continues to travel on the thoughts of repose.

Stone in Hand

Written on the petals of pure wit and white,
Seen only in the layers of day and night:

Tetragram: Stone and oil, steel and hand

The universe is conspiring to find you,
And find the others like you who choose to fight.
You've waged war on their reality and stand to feel something real.

*Tetragram: This is your quest. Has always been your quest.
Will forever be your quest, eternally.*

You hear the voice, big and small . . .
You know you will stand. Humanity depends on it.
Eternity is your faith. Forever is your place.

Stone and oil, steel and hand: tetragram.

Blade Out of Stone

I wonder . . . how many men would have tried in vane . . .
If Excalibur's blade came up from the hilt?

A blade out of rock; no handle to grasp;
Only sharp shiny steel to pull through and feel.

I wonder . . . how many fingers might lay at its base?
If those powerful men slid their hands around that place?

Would less test their strength? Would they see through themselves?
Knowing . . . the blade will cut through their lies.

Would the iron spire scribe a killing post . . .
For those mighty men to through all their foes?

Or, will gentle fingers finally find their reason . . .
From the hand of a man who has grasped the light inside.

The blade can see you through a ferrum cloud;
He can see you walking forward and reaching down.

We see you mirrored in our eyes—the sword comes free!
Together we will fight for truth—Veritas is our creed!

Live Oak Tree

What is that sound behind the trail behind us?
That slightly sighing rind of high-pitched forward?

There wasn't a chance I'd continue walkin' on,
And walking along the trail toward the mountaintop,
away from the play—I had to see her.

I turned around. I walked back down.
But there was nothing a' bound.
Not a squirrel. Not a bird. Just me and a tree—
Above the whistling-chiseling Creek.

I must agree, yes, I must assume the voice I heard was only me,
Taking a drink of Springtime's woodland breeze.

Then . . . I heard another sound repeat and beg me,
It said, please notice, don't go, don't leave.

The voice was coming from the creakin'
The squeakin' of an adolescent oak tree.

The breeze quickened to wind, and the leaves went wild;
Like a child on Easter Day, they went spinning,

through the branches, into new, unseen places;
Trying to hide—waiting for the right finder.

That day she found be blindly walking;
And under her arbor harbor she told me secrets:
She told me stories of long ago
And sung me songs of mornings yet had.

She, The Unseen Tree, knows what you and me,
and the leave struggle to see.

Peckerwood

There are three things in life I can say without strife
That my father did for me

The first is easy, he showed me a book,
He brought Robert Service to me;

Where the stories spin tales of the lonely trail,
And the men that don't fit in.

And if you ever get a chance to read about Sam,
Have a tear or two and grin

There are many things that swayed my ways,
Like sitting in the woods watching the birds:

It was their endless flight from the tree to the sky
From a pine full of holes—peckerwood holes,

Where the beetles flee the show . . .
From my mind this will never go.

Through their infinite flight of red, black, and white—
A woodpecker's dream come true.

And I'm layin' on a bench in the mountains, with my Pop
Our entertainers were all around.

Just don't make a sound,
And you might hear a cedar fall to the ground . . .

Is it a lumberjack's ghost . . . or a tree getting old?
May we never know.

I also liked his humorous side,
Sarcastic and funny to me.

But the best of these was the combination of three—
It was surprising alchemy.

For all things stirred, collected and cured,
Gave some to who I am.

Purity is a Dirty Word

Purity is the void unconnected, a world of its own,
A world wholly alone.

Surely purity is despised by those with any emotion,
It's made up of one and none.

Purity annuls beauty, it segregates part from part,
It eliminates the moon and the sun.

Certainly, purity is a dirty word, a pseudo-realm,
A place where nothing grows.

Beauty is the antithesis to the word that doesn't exist,
An opposite that is sure.

Beauty is mutually moving, touching, ensuing—love.
She is worth pursuing.

Beauty binds together all of our impure parts;
She is made from many.

Synergy inscribes her and drives her,
Makes her one. Makes us pure.

Diary of a Madman

October 3, 2014

Reality is a point along a spectrum of existence. I suggest ironically and relatively the point we are operating on is not inclusive of other perceptions available because we are all in a dream devoid of any senses that would suggest otherwise. And, just as in a dream, any thought that would come along to threaten this reality is quickly dissuaded and dismissed. Therefore we are living in a dream where our senses are dulled to the point of reality.

October 5, 2014

It's time to get the ball rolling for change in my life. My first step is to find . . . no, not find . . . it's already their. I need . . . I want to see the beauty in the truly beautiful. Like right now in the coffee shop, there is a young woman sitting across the table from me studying microbiology. She is wearing a necklace: the chain is gold and red and from it hangs a white crystal stone whose bottom half has several shades of green that seem to be creeping up though invisible veins.

After speaking with her I found that she had read <u>Don Quixote</u> in Spanish text. I should really continue reading his journey. Though, after reading the first few chapters of his and <u>look Homeward, Angel</u>, I've decided on Thomas Wolfe. I have to give credit, however, Miguel de Cervantes' preface is quite possibly the best I've ever read. Here's an excerpt:

> "I took, oftentimes, my pen in my hand to write it, and as often set it down again, as not knowing what I should write; and being once in a muse, with my paper before me, my pen in mine ear, mine elbow on the table, and mine hand on my cheek, imagining what I might write . . . "

October 7, 2014

Reading, <u>Look Homeward, Angel</u>, currently on chapter XIII, and I'm a bit annoyed. I want to hear more about Eugene rebelling against the social norms his siblings have accepted. I don't give a shit about his mother pursing her goddamned lips—like she has an original thought to share.

October 9, 2014

That great survivor of my happy mind has fallen through tall walls of tar to land on a feather bed of regret and loneliness. The peephole of hope is shrinking and while the light travels slowly darkness envelops my soul. Fear of insanity ebbs and flows equally today.

October 11, 2014

I had a dream last night where I was at the cusp of a jump from an airplane. There were other people in the plane whom did not know me, nor could I know them; I only knew it was time—my time. For a moment it was like a still picture was taken of the cargo hold and door, with me at the forefront of the shot and the three already falling from the door. I thought, "I might die today; but if I die, I die unafraid; and if I live, I will live on with a great victory."

I wrote a short rhyme about this dream:

ACDC rings her bells through propeller blades singing; He pulls the cord with no remorse though nothing comes along; No time to die—only death to see in darkness, truth, or dreams.

October 13, 2014

My dreams are merging with this reality; what was once a memory is now my conscious creation.

October 15, 2014

What lies have I told my secret heart? What virtues have died in a wake of lies? Maybe these questions aren't as important as the little changes we make everyday; the little choices, like the butterfly effect, will develop into great future changes.

October 17, 2014

Reading various old texts has inspired me to begin researching Latin: *Non bene pro toto libertas venditur auro*, Liberty is not well sold for all the gold. *Libertatem aut mortem*

Walking on Water October 19, 2014

I been thinking about this dream I had a few years ago—a strange dream . . . then . . . what dream doesn't seem strange while reflecting on it? Dreams never seem to have a beginning so much as they have a curtain that draws up allowing us to see the performance of our self both on and off a stage that morphs and changes with the minds fancy while, simultaneously and sometimes alternatively, looking through and into the sockets of our eyes.

I was in a large and empty room. There was a couch and a chair, and what was the outline of a kitchen somewhere to the upper right from my view. This kitchen seemed to be floating while stable, like a small particle surfs across the lens of your eye. I heard some noise through a door from the end of a short hallway. Being curious I went to see what it was. I opened the door and saw a child playing

in a room full of toys. The child was being watched by a tall stick figure who looked like a seven-foot tall pencil with arms. Another stickman appeared in the room and looked toward me; I sensed their intent here was not good. I crossed through the doorway with a rush and picked up the stickman nearest me and swung him like a baseball bat into the other. Sparks flew and wires showed through their skin colored tubing. Next I grabbed the child's hand and ran through the wall toward a harbor full of docks and boats.

By this time the stickmen were swarming everywhere; and, I had a group of children and a couple parents with me walking on the docks looking for a boat to flee from the invading robot-stick-men.

It was a large orange and white boat equipped with a galley when we boarded it in the harbor, and as we traveled away to the safety of the sea the people disappeared and the boat began to shrink and speed faster and faster. As this happened I saw myself from the perspective of my eyes and somewhere above that felt like having two sets of eyes with two sets of minds interpreting my surroundings. During this process, the me of the dream was intently talking an older man who, while driving the boat, grew older with its changing size.

They traveled alongside and past desert islands, tall and lonesome. Time speed up and stood still as they talked and traveled thousands of miles upon the sea. Then he was in control of the boat while the old man, who began to fade away, warned of the waves beginning to form from the direction of the starboard side.

He was alone while crashing waves headed toward his side threating to capsize the boat. He remembered something he had learned from his father long ago, "When waves begin to crash you must meet them head on and fast." He turned the boat ninety degrees to the right and accelerated. The first wave flung the boat into the air and back again into its absence. The second wave did the same as the first. And the third wave he traveled straight through. The boat continued to shrink rapidly, smaller and smaller and as he no longer fit in the boat he became tethered to it by a rope, like a man who skies on water with bare feet. Going faster and faster the boat shrank into nothingness, the waves and swells washed away into a clear and smooth surface of water.

He began to run on the waters surface. He was confused by this ability; but having seen it happening he embraced it. He ran deeper and deeper into the wilderness of the ocean, away from the dangers of land until he sped up to a new group of desert islands. He saw something shiny reflecting though the shallow water, and he stopped. Standing on water he stuck his head through the surface in order to see the shinning object; he dived down to sift his fingers through the sand and found some silver and gold coins he promptly stuck into his pocket, and an orange starfish who clung to his right hand.

Still below the water he looked out and saw a woman walking along the shore and in his direction—she was looking at him. The wind blew in the direction she was walking causing her dress to wrap around the slender curves of her body—she was beautiful in everyway. He swam up and stood upon the waters surface and looking toward her. She said to him, "This is not the treasure you are looking for. The treasure you seek is over there." She pointed away from the setting sun and he turned his back to her and walked in the direction she had pointed.

Sometimes I still see the me of this dream forever walking to into the east anticipating the arrival of his unknown treasure. What could this treasure be and when will I ever find it?

October 21, 2014

Why is it that around every corner I find someone saying that Latin is a dead language? Taxonomy, science, art, literary classics are works of art still alive and pumping through the veins of those who still hold art in their heart.

Although some will say that Latin is dead . . . if that be true all great literature is doom to be enigmas. Knowledge lost, our souls forever locked away and dying—forever seeking quid est veritas.

October 23, 2014

Beauty is felt as sensation of all the senses filling my soul with senseless awe.

September 27, 2015

About six years ago, after the end of a long relationship, I began an experiment. This experiment involved many interpersonal studies I found in social media, acquaintances, friends, family, and romantic involvements. In fact, this experiment involved every aspect of my life, every aspect save for one: my daughter; she was the only part of my life safe from manipulation for the sake of experimentation.

Because this experiment was in regard to all those around me I deemed myself as the primary manipulator and the control. In hindsight I was more like a mad-scientist, as my methods were based more in lunacy than science. Even still, this process yielded some unexpected results; however long it did take to realize. The primary and most personal section of this experiment asked the questions: what is love and how does it exist? And, if it does, does anyone else know of this?

First I began my studies through retrospection, reflection, and research. I asked myself, "Did I ever love anything or anyone? Have I ever exemplified love?" The me of six years ago could not answer those questions, as he knew not what love was. Though, what ensued was a psychosis that would take several years to overcome.

He began to read book, after novel, after essay trying to gain knowledge toward understanding more on any topic he could and with the relationships he entered into he did so with a certain serious matter-of-fact-ness, unbeknownst to those involved. In these interactions he would create a hypothesis with the use of a single variable being given or taken away; the results only added to his matter-of-fact-ness and confidence he wielded—he was lost in his fancy of knowledge—he became so completely enamored with his newfound knowledge, he lost track of the purpose of his experiment.

He researched chemistry, physics, and many things natural within them: quarks, atoms, molecules, organisms, ecosystems, planetary interactions; from sub-atomic to the atom-bomb, micro through macro and back again; through times of cultures past, present, and trending future; plays of the terrestrial and the divine. He searched to cosmos for answers and found none that would make clear love's place in conscious thought. And, as he gave up on his quest to understand he began to remember his experiments he started years ago. He thought how foolish he was to think he could understand something as sacred as the idea of love. Until, one night he saw two lights in the sky that caused him to watch and contemplate their movements over the course of time. They helped him think more simply. And, from this, he wrote a poem of two planets chasing one another, like they were dancing; yet, he still had not grasped the understanding of love.

He thought he was on the path of love-less-ness, giving up on love; or, the idea of it anyway. "Sure," he thought, "atoms and planets do it. Everything in nature does it. Why can't I? Maybe it's just not in the scope of human ability to bond within the principles of physical universe; maybe humans are the exception to the rule." Then it dawned on him, "there is more than love operative in universe. The answer is in the basic Principle of Love: since love cannot be expressed alone love cannot exist without its antithesis." He realized while he was searching to understand love he had been resisting its possibility countless times because he was, deep down, afraid. He continued to ponder The Principle of Love, "Love is the force created between propulsion and repulsion. Like protons, neutrons, and electrons . . . like planets dancing through the sky at night. The key to love must be in allowing the dance . . .

He continued to contemplate the process of his flawed experiment and the naivety he operated it on, "All the thinking . . . all the knowledge . . . all the research . . . all the possibilities now impossible! All to arrive at a principle of such simplicity. Ah . . . the universe, she is a bitch." What he did not know is that his tenacity, however misplaced it became along the path to love, would express in the steps of the dance to come.

September 28, 2015

I watched the lunar eclipse last night. It was the most spectacular harvest moon I'd ever seen, turning the moon a dull red. Interestingly, the last time the moon went through a total eclipse at perigee was the same year I was born.

This brings back memories of my mother and some things she had shared with me long before she had passed away . . . she told me that when I was a baby I got sick a lot and I never had a fever. Over several months the doctors who saw me could not understand how I could be so sick and not produce a fever, they couldn't figure out what was causing this. She was driving us home from yet another doctor visit and praying to god . . . praying that whatever was wrong with me be healed. That night she saw what she said was the brightest moonrise she'd ever seen. The very next day I had a fever and became a normal healthy baby. To this day the doctors could not explain what was wrong with me or how I got better. My mother said god answered her prayer and I'm inclined to agree.

I wonder if the moon my mother saw was like the moon I watched last night . . . I wonder if it eclipsed sometime during the night . . . I wonder if those same celestial forces changed reality . . . and will they change things today . . .

September 29, 2015

My world has definitely changed. The future is full of a world I couldn't have imagined in my wildest dreams. The future is an open book with infinite pages for me to write, to color, to play . . . to laugh and to live . . . and to share my pen and my book with those I love.

February 1, 2016

    I don't know if this continued dream sensation is taking place over a period of time, years maybe, or a single nights' sleep. Could it be that these dream memories only seem to be a repetition of some sort? Or, are these memories secret realities that remain unspoken by those who remember?

    The dreams might be a completely different reality simply being contrary to the current paradigm; or it could be that what I see is contrary to what should be.

    These feelings remind me of a poem I read a while back: " . . . dreams of love, amity, and desire, dreams by the fire, visions in waves and haunts; dreams where her and I are mutually sought, caught by the bond of a mystic wand.'

    Whatever the truth may be, the reality of my dream seems to be that my heartstrings are pulling my soul in impossible directions. Or is it my soul strings pulling my heart . . .

The River of Israel

The Highway

William hopped into his car, if you'd call it that: Izzy's car is an old Volkswagen bus. One with sun-faded-brittle orange and white zigzag lined curtains trailing the windows, a single pot cooktop, a small sink controlled by a grimy white plastic hand pump lever mounted above an ice box full of cobwebs, and a faded orange vinyl convertible bed covered by old wool blankets. In the middle below the louvered window the table is folded out—as it often is during the day. Bed, table, and drivers' seat, Izzy is always at one of these.

On the table a checkerboard is painted red and black; though Izzy is much more fond of chess. When Izzy was nine he discovered he could play chess alone—along with other strategic games where the only secrets were in the mind.

Not card games though; card games relied on bluffs and hiding truths. Izzy was not interested in that. Izzy wanted to understand . . .

William put the key into the ignition and then with a twist of the wrist he sent the gears of the starter in motion. The pistons in the engine began to move through their magnesium case like an organ breathing in and out cold and hot flames of fire and air. He grabbed onto the eight ball spinner mounted on the steering wheel and turned left out of the drive onto a winding red dirt road. A creek littered with cottonwood and sycamore trees followed the road in a wake of dust flung from the new radial tires. The wheels, and the rest of this vehicle, are another question: the white paint on the steel wheels had begun to bubble and flake off after last winter. Now, rust bubbles through the cracks, and it shoots out orange-red dust with the slightest poke of a curious finger. Oil leaks though the head gaskets, in to and out of the cylinders, causing a white smoke with a slight blue tint to puff rings through the lingering air. The rings of smoke seem to float in the dust as it drifts through the trees and over the creek—the smoke looks like little ringed ghosts that seem to smile in the drift in the wake of their trail. Below the bunk the valves and rods combined and chittered a rhythmic chatter of a well-tuned baby grand.

William looked at Izzy, squinting his eyes at the evening sun, "hey pal, is this rust bucket gunna hold together? I mean it'd be real pain in the ass to push it back home, don't you think?"

"She'll make it wherever we need to go. Old faithful. Ha ha! Old faithful Betsy, that's what she is. She's been through rivers and over mountains a million times! She'll drive in and out of many more!"

The yellow orange two-tone van bobbed over the bumps in

the road like a boat floating headlong behind breaking waves into high and wide rolling folds following a long-shore current. The suspension is shot but the springs are wound tight, and lifts the cab higher toward the sky. This van, bus, whatever you might call it is a vessel of many uses: transportation, a haven, and a home for Izzy to roam from place to place. Though, really, he has never roamed very far from his hometown. The local mountains and the beach . . . sure, but a hundred miles or more would seem unfathomable to him. Izzy *has* had the idea of driving away from his little town in The South: drive to the *other* coast where he would leave Betsy behind and find a ship headed for the Channels of other lands. Something kept him from traveling far, though; something he doesn't understand. Fear.

"Where are we headed William?"

"On an adventure! An epic adventure to the moon and the sun: a journey for all mankind. One small step for Izzy, and one giant leap for William! Ha ha!

"William, Highway 9 isn't exactly a giant leap for one either of us and cows don't really jump over the moon. Where are we headed?"

"Ah, but gymnasts can, and birds and bats fly over the moon day and night. Oh, and kids on bikes with strange little aliens do, too. Stars *do* shoot through the sky and *you and I* are going to, as well. Maybe not in the literal sense, but we will do it. People will see us fly over the moon and the sun; from the right vantage point, that is."

"I hope their vantage point isn't somewhere behind us, at the moment all they'll see is smoke and dust. What are you trying to tell me Will?"

"Izzy, you trust this rust bucket. Trust me. I'll get us where we need to go."

A song came on the radio. A song by Jimi Hendrix, "The Wind Cries Mary." William turned the sound up a bit and the wind whispered a tale, through the dashboard vents of a king and queen without a name.

Izzy remained very quiet. And so did William. They continued to drive south down highway 9: a dusty red and winding dirt road headed *nowhere*. Izzy thought about what William had said, he thought about a shooting star, he wondered what it'd look like if he could jump up to the moon and catch one, he wondered if he might bump into a gymnast on his way to the moon, he wondered if he would meet a girl with blue-hazel eyes . . . or, were they gold-hazel . . . maybe all of these spiraled through green . . . He fell asleep into his thoughts and the sound of pebbles flinging from the tire treads.

We hug the road, we fling the rocks; we grip the dust and send it flyin'. The ground is ours, the land we scar; we find and grind and lead the way. The rail's the same, no tracks remain; the rubble tears the rubber tears. We'll roll for you; go round the world for you—108, the sun away.

Izzy slept: his head against an old rolled up wool coat between him and the vibrations of the window. William continued to drive south on highway 9 through the night, driving toward a myriad of stars over the horizon: a flat land, a desert land of sand and rocks, open space in a landscape lost by time, hundreds of miles away from the red dirt road, ready for a night camp in the deserted wilderness.

William shifted down the gears of the old VW bus, and pumped the brakes slowly as he did so. The road turned sharply to the east. The brake shoes finally grabbed their drums lending the old transmission to rest. William made the turn and stopped the rolling wheels; he stepped out leaving Izzy to sleep and thought of the adventure ahead that Izzy knew nothing about and he *too* knew little of. Only that they were on the road: the road of living. William hunkered down and laid on the soft desert sand by the side of the road looking up to summer's moonless stars and drifted to sleep. The stars sat in the background patently waiting.

Through the night the hot air from the driver's side radial tires babbled and ebbed with a silent whisper, the air and steam percolated out where the rubber met the rim's seam. A slither of steam moved out and condensed into beads of water on the inner white walls and nestled up inside the wheel's wells, hiding from the sun to come. *The sun will giveth and the sun will taketh away those precious things the moon hast bayed.*

"William! William! Wake up! The coyotes. Can you hear them?"

"Yes, Izzy, I heard them in my dream; *I saw* them in my dream. There was a battered old ranch south of the bend with a gravel drive by its porch. It was weird . . . a cow was giving birth just before daybreak and the coyotes were circling the . . . soon to be

mother—the soon to be grieving cow. I saw the calf's birth. The coyotes tore it apart—almost pulled it from his mother's womb. The dream stopped when you said my name."

"I dreamt of the stars—. Coyotes! I woke up to the coyote's cries from the south. William, that isn't all . . . the tires are flat. Both the left tires are flat!" *The new radial tires . . . ?* Izzy thought.

"Let's walk south, Izzy. I have a strange felling we'll find something."

Water, William thought. *We will need water.* They knew Highway Nine was not often traveled and why they didn't bring more water did not make sense. Maybe they thought of the vehicle only: this machine did not run on water, nor did it need water for cooling, this bus was air-cooled. The bus was old reliable. The bus, like Izzy had said, would make it wherever they needed to go. *Make it.* Izzy thought as he opened the side sliding door, jerking the handle free from its latch and catch. He grabbed his backpack and a canteen of water then gently slammed the door shut. He pulled out a small pad of paper, like the ones used by detectives in old time crime stories, and a pencil from the top of his beige pack and wrote a note—he placed it on the windshield:

"Two flat tires. Only one spare. Walking south toward . . ."

Jacob Burnard

The House

    They left the bus parked at the start of highway 6 and walked south. They walked toward William's dream and Izzy's recollection, south, where highway nine had ended; where highway nine *might* continue.

    The desert was flat and the sun began to blaze, it was only eight in the morning by the time they covered seven miles, drinking the rest of their water from an old canteen: an old beat up aluminum canteen Izzy had gotten from his father years ago. Izzy was thirteen when his father began to tell him stories of the war, of Vietnam, the war that should-never-have-been. During that same time, his father began training him in the ways of combat and survival, of guerrilla warfare: how to stay hidden, setting traps for humans and animals alike, looking for the usefulness of rocks on the ground, looking for the slightest drop in topography, looking for anything that might become a necessity, of inventing new ways to do things, looking. But, most importantly, overcoming by sheer force of will.

    Izzy had learned to travel at dawn and dusk of desert light, and sometimes in the dead of night. So many skills he had been taught not knowing why his father was teaching these to him. Some Izzy simply enjoyed for the bond they created for his father and him, some because it was fun, and others because he felt it would prove himself a man.

"William, I see something ahead. It looks like a house,

William showed a crooked grin and pat Izzy on the back. They continued walking toward the small house: grey sharp gravel led up to the steps leading up to a patio with no shade for deck—no shade for anything, save for it's north facing side that might hide the walls from the sun at eleven and one o'clock. The boards were worn grey and creaked under their feet. The heads of the nails seemed to pop up and greet them as the boards bowed below with each step. The home was white with a flaking grey-blue fascia. A single wind chime hung next to the front door—silent.

"I don't like the looks of this place; it reminds me of a dream I had last year." Izzy remarked with concern.

"Good. We are going to this house. If it reminds you of a dream we should most definitely see what this lonely house is all about."

"Okay, William, Maybe we could find some water."

William has always been one for adventure and remembering. Izzy was one of the contemplating types: logical. Together, they made a great pair. Together they walked up to the house. Together they walked up the creaking steps and knocked on the door. No one answered. There was not a single vehicle to be seen. There were no trees. There was just this house, alone. William reached for the door latch, depressed it with his thumb and slowly pushed the white door open. The house was empty. Except for the yellowish walls and dark brown carpet, empty. There was not even a kitchen inside. This was an old house, a very old house.

"How about that? William said sarcastically, looks like they packed up and left. Packed up everything *except for this?*"

William picked up a strange object from the carpet; an odd object about 3 inches big and layered with dust, William held it out toward Izzy, "what do you make of this?"

"Looks like a gyroscope. My dad had one . . . *has one?*"

"What's it for? Looks like it's made from gold. Valuable?"

"Valuable, yes, but it's not gold: it's used to balance things like rockets and ships. Not this one, exactly. This one is more of a tool used to teach the principles of balance in motion to children. Other things, too, but I can't recall all of them. I'm going to see if there is a well around back."

There was a well: one of those old cast iron hand pump type. There was a chain around it and the handle, with an old master lock, *master link*, linking the winding figure eights of the chain around the pump shaft and handle. Thankfully, Izzy always carried a hatchet, a large hatchet, you could probably call and axe. He's had it since his teens, always had it on every adventure.

His father, seemingly long ago, often criticized Izzy for bringing the axe along on their backcountry trips: trips that lead into the wilderness for miles, carrying everything on their backs. His father thought that weight, if he was going to carry more weight than necessary, should be for carrying more water, especially on their desert trips where water was scarce. *Water*, Izzy thought.

Izzy had used his hatchet-axe as a sort of multi-tool: chopping wood, hammering, digging, as a weapon if needed, even entertainment. During the shady moments of noontime while his father napped on the ground on an old military wool blanket, a blanket stuck with small twigs and sticks and burs, with holes that showed the love of a moth, a grateful moth, who in this wool blanket found redemption from his plight of having to find food and shelter. During these moments Izzy would hack at things. Taking eight paces from a tree he would turn swiftly trying to stick the blade end of the axe head in the hard bark of an old oak or pine tree. Sometimes Izzy would twirl the handle around, occasionally throwing it into the air with a spin and try to catch it. The axe head caught Izzy more times than Izzy caught the handle—cutting and bruising his hands. But, the times he caught it flawlessly erased the memory of the scars. Time erased those scars, as well, most of them, anyway. Izzy didn't mind the scars because to him they showed his achievements. He revered his blade but was not afraid of it—at least, he wasn't afraid of it when he was a young man, when he was fifteen. Izzy was nineteen now, as was William. Nineteen. And, while he had learned a little bit more about the guiles of adulthood, he was still a young man, younger than he though himself to be.

Why would anyone chain up a well in the desert? Water. Why lock up water? Why lock up a well? Izzy continued to contemplate. It didn't make sense. *Water is not an object to own and lock away. Water, from the earth, why?* Izzy put his right hand behind himself and reached to the bottom of his pack, he unbuttoned the head of his axe from its sheath and let the back of the axe head slip through his fingers, slowly; midway down the hickory handle he began to tighten his grip, slowly, like an engineer braking a train to a stop at station, His hand found the perfect grove, clasped on, and swiftly swung the axe down, out, and up into the air. He swung the old rusty axe with violent precision and hit the old rusted lock, hit it hard and true; it broke free the link in the chain—broke free the link that may have been hiding this water for fifty or a hundred years, or more. Izzy unwrapped the chain and pulled on the lever but it was rusted tight. He wedged the axe handle between the lever and well shaft and popped the rust from its hinges. Izzy pumped and pump the lever up and down but nothing came, not even air. *Maybe the well is dry . . . or maybe, just maybe it only needs to be primed.* Izzy left the well to get William. Izzy had an idea.

William was sitting on the floor over a bare spot in the carpet spinning the gyroscope like a top, staring at it, staring into it, lost in a daze of its movement—going every which way and going nowhere—spinning. *Like a dog chasing its tail.* The gyroscope stopped spinning and fell as Izzy walked in.

"William, tell me you haven't gone pee yet. Tell me you need to go. The well seems dry but it's not. I know it."

"What? Izzy, what are you talking about? "

"The well. Out back. I broke the lock and pumped the lever but nothing came out. I think the pipe needs a prime. We could use our pee to fill the pump. I don't know if it will be enough but it's worth a try. It's burning hot out here, must be 118 degrees."

Izzy always carried a small pouch in his pack with certain items, small items, which might prove useful under many conditions. This was a condition he was not completely familiar with; but he knew the well was old and that with wells like this, they relied on suction. The handle was loose and air did not come through with pumping. *Seals, old rubber seals, like chapped lips, will not do the trick.* Izzy did not want to waste their valuable liquids on a failed attempt so he reached into his pouch and pulled out a small-capped cylinder, it was a used Rx bottle filled with cotton balls and petroleum jelly. He popped the cap open, stuck his right index and middle finger in and removed a swab of the jelly. William and Izzy carefully emptied the contents of their bladder into the wells spigot, listening to it as it leaked into the shaft. Izzy breathed in the musky smell of damp iron as he reached inside the spigot with two fingers gooped in the jelly and lathered it everywhere he could reach—reaching desperately toward all the round corners and edges inside, savoring the taste of silver and steel from the roof of his mouth.

"All right. William, push the handle down slowly so the lube will smooth out inside and seal the walls. Then continue to pump up and down just like you pump the brakes in old Betsy—but don't stop! This is our only chance at getting any water."

William pumped the handle up and down. The *water* gurgled inside. *Was it going down or coming up?* Both. Within several seconds dark rusty water began to sputter and flow out of the spigot.

"For the love of god: Will, don't stop pumping the handle. We might not get another chance at this."

William continued to pump for several minutes, minutes that seemed like days. After a while the water became more and more clear with every swing. The water pooled up around the pump. The water from the spigot became clear—crystal clear. Izzy held the canteen under the flowing water and filled it up. Next, he submerged his head, wetting his hair and gulping the running water copiously. He filled his belly, hair, and clothes with as much water as he could—

drenched his wool coat in it, too. Izzy came to a stand and took over pumping the lever while William bathed in the flowing water. Izzy, grateful, rummaged through his pack and pulled out a necklace, beaded through with hollow bone and a amazonite pendant, one his father had given him. He placed it on the well with a gesture of thanks.

The two walked away from the blazing sun and back into the house. It was about four o'clock. William was curious about the dream Izzy had mentioned. The dream about the house, *what was it that Izzy didn't like? Why was Izzy afraid of remembering?* Izzy sat down, leaning against the yellow wall. William sat to his right against the adjoining wall, below a place where a picture once hung, judging by the lighter color of yellow in the shape of a square. Or . . . maybe it was a mirror, a small mirror.

"Izzy, what was that dream about? The one you mentioned earlier."

"I told you about that dream once before. I share all my dreams with you, most of them, anyway."

Would your share this with me once again?

Izzy sighed. "Yes, William, I will share it with you, once more. It will seem strange, eerie, even. I had this dream about a year after my mom died, about six months ago. I'm telling you Izzy, it's weird."

"Let's here it." William said in an air of empathetic excitement.

"I was driving through the desert in the old Chevy pickup I

used to have. It seemed like I was driving for days, weeks, maybe. I had no idea why I was driving or where I was driving, only that I knew I had to keep on going. The highway was paved, unlike highway Nine, but old. There was a bend in the road that turned left. Straight ahead of the bend I saw a house down a dirt road. I remember feeling compelled, driven, to drive straight toward that house, so I did. I pulled up into the half-moon gravel drive, walked up the steps to the door and rang the doorbell. There was a screen door, but the main door was wide open. I could see through the screen door and directly ahead there was a hallway leading straight through the house with open empty rooms on the right and the left before the halls opening. From a doorway on the left side of the hall my grandfather walked out and turned to see me with a great smile."

Izzy's grandfather was a large man, a tall man that commanded a quiet presence of strength in heart, mind, and seldom but sometimes necessary, voice. Izzy never knew his grandfather to be able to walk; his grandfather was aging with polio. When Izzy was four years old, on visits to see his grandfather, Rich and him played card games: war and go fish, Izzy cherished those times, his grandfather was kind and smiled all the time; at least, in all the times Izzy was aware of. Rich continued to age and the polio became worse: his ability to speak and move was near nothing by the time Izzy was thirteen. Soon after, Izzy's grandfather's heart stopped suddenly one afternoon. Rich was Izzy's mother's stepfather. He never had any children of his own; but he had grandchildren he cherished every moment with—his undivided attention, love, and interactions proved that.

"William, I smiled. I smiled ear to ear; at least that is what I felt. My granddad invited me in; he seemed press to show me something exciting. I followed him down the hall and into the room. There were shelves with books and knickknacks surrounding me everywhere. There was the old bar and bar chair he sat at when we played cards, and the tall directors chair I would sit in, making me feel like a king, being three. He took some items off the shelf, one after the other, and showed them to me. I don't remember . . . or, I couldn't make out what they were. I was just excited to see him, to see him walking and talking in my dream. I think I knew it was a dream. Finally, he said, "I have something else to show you." He walked out of the room back toward the front door—I followed. In the room, the empty room, my mother appeared. She was standing, wearing her favorite quilted coat and white leggings—holding a book. I walked to her smiles. She handed me the book. I looked at it: a blank cover page. I opened it and there were words written in the first few pages—but the rest was blank, many pages with no writing. I was confused. The book seemed to vanish. I looked at my mom. She looked at me. And we embraced with joy: hugging and holding each other. Soon, I looked down and saw her feet: her swollen feet in her white tied shoes. Suddenly I was sure this was a dream and we began to weep. I cried. Mom embraced me. She cried, too. It was hurting our hearts as I began to know that she was going to die.

Then, I knew she was already dead. She held me in her arms—I felt her embrace reach into me. My dream ended and I woke up immediately. William, I woke up to my AM/FM radio alarm clock playing a song, "In the Arms of an Angel." I cried all morning. That was the day I stopped going to my college classes. That was the day I bought Betsy."

William looked at Izzy with wet eyes. William walked to Izzy and embraced him. The welling tears broke free and tears streamed freely to one another—for one-another. They didn't speak. And after a while they laid down on the brown carpet—thinking: thinking about one another, thinking about the turns that life threw a child and a man. Thinking, and exhausted by emotions, they fell to sleep.

There is something strange to say for loved ones gone to the grave . . . .

The Town

    Sunlight began shinning through a crack in a boarded up window that beamed down on Williams face in a line across his eyes. He looked like an Inuit wearing snow goggles, due to his thick dark lashes rising like bristle cone pine spires from the edge of his eyelids. William blinked slowly, breathing in a candy-pine scent, squinting from the sun, still blurry and red eyed from the night before. He had seen through Izzy's eyes, he saw the grief welling inside those bright blue eyes: grief for his mother lost and gone, grief for the life that haunted ahead. Grief and fear, alone, to deal with the tortures of his mind.

    William knew how to help his friend. He knew that compassion and remembering where the keys. He knew that time was also needed. But not too much time—just the right amount—stages of time.

    William sat up and said Izzy's name in a questioning way. But there was no response. *Maybe he's outside?* Izzy was always an early riser, he knew. William got to his feet, groggy, and wandered outside toward the well. Izzy's pack was on the ground near the well, wet with murky water, but he was nowhere to be seen. Some dusted foot tracks led southeast toward the mountains. William was confused. *Where had Izzy gone? Why?*

"Izzy! Izzy!" *Where the hell'd you run off to?*

William shouldered Izzy's pack, he stared into the amazonite dangling from the pump, thinking about the deep colors in its hold, he lifted the stone and draped it over his head and it fell down onto his neck. William followed the worn footsteps leading toward the mountains. He walked with the wind to his back: blowing, eroding the desert hard pack into rising winds, bringing the dust from the tracks into the sky like a cold snow flurry blowing a snowflake from shady holes in the ground, only to settle down in some other place and melt into the earth on a hotter day when it would seep down a mineral spire of a dark-cold cave—hidden are the journeys a drop of clear water makes; until it carries something with it, the face of water is thirsty for . . .

If only the desert-hot-dust were snow to melt William might have some repose. Though, if something is not hot, it is cold. A river either flows or is frozen. And the snow has its own set of rules. William knew these things. He also knows that solidity is a matter of perception—that cold and hot are degrees of relations to things he doesn't fully understand.

William walked in the fading footsteps left by Izzy's boots. Walking deeper into the desert of desolate need to meet his friend on the trail that Izzy, for some reason, chose to go without warning. Was there something about remembering the dream of his mother that spurred him on some want of a lonely walk? *Would Izzy simply begin walking back to the house and see William on the way?* William had a feeling something was out of the ordinary. Somehow he knew that he must follow these footsteps. Somehow, William knew that he would find Izzy on the other side of a mountain. The Far Mountain.

The sun was raging over a town up ahead in a bend. There he saw Izzy's fading footsteps leading straight toward the mountain, south. But this town: old, older than the house: buildings of bare wood, old and grey, left to the sun and wind; and a pile of white bricks on the left bank of the hard-pack road. Surly, like the house, this place must be abandoned. And yet, William was curious. He veered away from Izzy's steps and began to walk down the rubble street of this ghost town.

William heard a sound . . . footsteps . . . like the town is coming alive . . . click-clack, click-clack . . . Boots on the boardwalk a vulture on the pine. Tick, tock, the clock strikes noon. *A clock? Where?* William's thoughts are confused, yet, suddenly alert. Then, with a crack!

The spin of her six shot turned his head toward her sights. It's a gleamin'; she's a glarin', down that long colt 45 . . .

Looking around and screaming, William shouts "Where the hell am! What is this!"

She has come to claim you! She is the minstrel, the muse, and the lady of anguish—The Siren of Sonora! Her eyes have found you, they've found their way to into your soul . . . *Maybe she's an angel—but she might be the Reaper . . .*

William is in disbelief. "What just happened? Where am I?

What is this?" *Heat stroke, a dream, purgatory*—? A many number of thoughts flow through William's mind; he knows, whatever the case may be, he is here and the time is now. Tock . . . tock . . . tock . . . the clock is cocked.

Another voice beckons. *"Snap out of it!* You've been caught, she has got you—it's time for your fight . . . It's you she wants, and she won't stop lookin'

William peeked through a hole in the bearskin and saw the beauty in her eyes, in her lips, in her want and need. She truly is a wonderful scene. She wants you, Will. She needs you—for a mate. To fall into her and this place—fall together, for a moment that will put my name in the turbid-hedron of mirrored faces.

She is The Sonoran Queen. William you are here for her. She is the queen of deserted lands, known by many names stakes claim to a wanderer's hand. She speaks sweetly into his eyes and soul and mind.

"But I am no wanderer. I'm looking for my friend."

You've wandered, Will. You've wandered but a few steps toward her. She wants you. She talks to you. She stalks your soul. Hear her call:

"I will show you love and give you lust. My splendor will enmesh and test you. Leave your dreams, leave your friend and follow me . . . Love and lust are one to us. Come with me. Trust in me. Love in me. All you wish to do— do in me. The dreams you share with me, the dreams of her—I am she. I am the one you want. I am the one you need. Sacrifice will. Blow your thoughts and dreams like dust from the boots on your feet. I am here. I am now. I am she who you seek. See me! Stare into my eyes once more. You'll know it's true.

Take into my bosom; take into my breath the sweet honey dew-drops of fallen green leaves upon your head."

The town has changed. The buildings are new with paint and signs and swinging doors. Horses are hitched at the saloon and bank. Men are walking from place to place—smiling in a solemn pace—waiting patiently for the return of Will's lost face.

William hears thoughts that are not his: a thought of a man's much coarse than his own. *What are you doing? You Dupe! Turn around! Your eyes are stronger than her! You are Vilhelmus Filius Vis! You are here to face her. Return her to the dirt of this desert land. Kiss her sweetly then stomp her into the sand. Do not dither any longer.* Stand.

The town's become silent and still. They're waiting for the fight, or the submission of his will. Men with faded faces facing William's gaze stay waiting on the boardwalk in front of the bank and bar. Women wearing white satin dresses stay wanting through black iron curtains from second story windows waiting for another faded face to line the boardwalk pine.

William gets up and smiles, not knowing why, knowing he must, and walks toward her. Walking slowly and happily toward his queen.

She is the queen, William; She will always be the queen—your queen. She is strong as you are strength. She is the one you want. "Sonora. Yes," William says in a slow hiss. "I *do* want her." Walking closer and closer with his arms to his sides and his palms facing out. She is smiling. Her grinning lips are kinked to the right—showing her passions wrinkle up her nose and her right eye. Sonora holsters her steel and takes a step forward, awaiting his embrace.

How many men the same has she trapped in her gaze? How many men have been slain by her love and her gun? How many men have been slain by his wanting hands? The answer is clear, as she is still here: every single one.

Tick . . . Tick . . . Tick . . . The trigger is locked. She sees his lips, she sees the truth, and trusts in his eyes. She thrusts herself onto him, wanting him, touching him, loving him. William's palms embrace her face, his fingers slide through her hair; his eyes glide into her stare. *He did not try to run like the others . . .* she thinks. *He is mine. I've finally found him . . . I've found the one with a face.* William hears her thoughts.

"Yes, my queen, you are my love. You are the queen of my heart. But you are not complete, nor am I. I must travel on and find my friend. I will see you again."

Regina is clinging to him. She sees the truth in his eyes. She is crying. William holds her face in his hands. He kisses her passionately on the forehead. Her face turns into fine-filed sand and runs down to the ground in a gleam of glass, the image of her fading face, of her eyes, looking up and falling down, engraved into his mind. She thought she'd found him. She did find him. She reached her left hand out in hopes that he'd reach back and keep her. He let her go to blow with the desert sand. William fainted to the ground.

William stammers up and questions his sanity wondering what had just happened to him—*heat stroke.* He seems to know; yet he does not. *Izzy, I have got to find Izzy. How long have I been lying in the dirt?*

The sun is straight overhead. William got up to his feet and brushed the sun shining sand from his lips, tasting the minerals and feeling the grit as he did so. He looked over his shoulder and saw a holstered gun laying in the sand. Without a second's thought he strapped the belt on and slid the gun and holster to his left hip and walked back to Izzy's steps. Where Izzy's steps had been. But they are gone—the wind blew them away.

The mountains are closer now, closer than he had thought. He can see the alluvium spread below a canyon of the mountain's highest peak: snow cap-spired and ridged. William knows this is the way Izzy is headed. He knows there may be water in the canyon: a stream or a spring to get a drink. But, it is hot in the noon sun and the mountain must be another 12 miles away. He is hungry, tired, and chapped. William wouldn't make it in the heat of midday. Well, maybe he could, but patience will serve better than guts.

William found some shade back in the ghost town in front of what was once a saloon. He sat against the wall, pack still on, and stretched his legs out straight in front of him, right foot over left. He wondered about the white pile of bricks and thought about the three little pigs . . . *Why would a bank of bricks fall to the ground and a bar of wood stay standing? Bricks are stronger than sticks and grass . . . I thought. Unless the bank, or was it a jail, was the target of someone's destruction.* William continued to ponder the possibilities of this nursery rhyme being wrong. *Could a wood structure hold up better to the huffing and puffing of a wolf's breath? Against the wind, are bricks and mortar weaker than planks and nails? Maybe.* The wind erodes many things; but wolves are not as patient. Other creatures may be.

The Sonoran Queen no longer rules this land. She is but a young cowgirl in the sand kneeling at his feet and incomplete.

The Bank

Rewind the spiraled brass-blue hands of time wrought to move and remind you of a child lost and gone. Gone from memory and remembered by mind—the heart cannot forget the anguish of a child slain for another man's sake.

William woke up. The Sun is passing beyond The Far Mountains. William remembers that it's time to find Izzy. The wind is cooler and the stars are coming to life. The Moon is beginning to peer through the flat lands of the east while a wolf howls from the south.

Clink . . . Plink . . . Scrape . . . William looked over to his right as the broken white bricks came back to life, stacking with the scratch of a trowel in invisible hands while iron bars in rows of first story windows rose up from the dust of rust in the ground. The wood-steel door is hung in front, latched and locked.

William, you must stand. William shook his head softly with a blink and got to his feet. He saw the bank brought back to new. Startled, he remembered the holster and the gun strapped to his left hip, and reached for the driftwood grips and lifted out a large brass key. His eyebrows came down, not to a complete squint, but his face is postured in a questioning way. For some reason it is easier to believe that bricks and buildings can come to life, more so than it is for a gun to transform into a key. But William can see a door at the bank: he can see the lock and keyhole. . . He began to see a vision of himself standing at the bar and entering a steel riveted wood plank door of the bank.

"Whose eyes brought this simple vision to me? Whose spell brought the bank into new? Who replaced the gun with a key?" William looked down at the amazonite pendant dangling from his neck and rolled it through his thumb and fingers, he walked toward the steel door.

William slid the key effortlessly into its home and turned it to the right, slowly, hearing the sound of brass rubbing steel—feeling the teeth grind on the turning wheel inside sent shivers up his spine. He is weary. . . has a hunch that whatever lay behind this door is something he's not ready for, something he does not want to see.

Curiosity killed the cat without a hat, the cap passed on to top the inquisitive man without a mind; the minds he finds he sucks them dry to fill his head—to create the brain he does not have. His name is Nemo. He has no soul and still he walks these lands— his hands never let go.

Curiosity is not the force driving William through the door—it's more like a magnet suddenly changed polarity and is pulling him in that direction; like gravity with a thought to share in an electric pulse.

He must pass through the fulcrum of the door . . . a threshold holding fresh the flesh left behind by the man without a mind—left locked up in a prison to live alone and scared—trapped in a dark room with walls of white bricks.

William pushed the door slowly and walked across the threshold into a large dark room. The door closed slowly behind him and latched with a click. He thought about the door being closed, and as he is poised into darkness he is unconcerned; because, ahead in the center of the vault he sees a dim light ebbing and emanating from a small figure seated in a chair, like a firefly caught in a jar and about to die.

William stopped. He suddenly had a sense of déjà vu or a dream remembered. A dream he does not know but still can see the entire show right before his eyes of a little girl sitting in an old wooden chair with her wrists bound with rope to the curved arms of a pine chair. The girl seated must me eight or nine years old; and there seems to be another little girl of six or seven years dancing just beyond the focus of his periphery. In this dream, he or another man walks up to the bound girl and notices her throat lightly cut; a wound not bleeding but open to the air. *Nemo, this must be Nemo's dream . . .* William questions with disgust. And, as he, as this man walked up to the little bound girl he lifted his right hand up only to see a serrated knife in its grip. He walked right in front of the little girl; she is still awake and alert, seemingly unafraid. He was holding the knife and wonders, *did I do this to her?* He looked at her thinking she is sure to die from her wounds. He thought he must put her out of her pain, like a dying animal suffering on the side of the road. He walked up to her. She is unafraid. He looked straight into her eyes as he grinded and carved the knife deeper into her little neck making sure to cut through the carotid arteries. The unskilled and jagged cuts begin to ooze blood sending it to run down her neck and arms— spiraling down the spindles of the chair. She looked up at him and said, *You are doing this because you want me to be like you.* He thinks, *what have I done?* And wakes up.

The light in the room is flickering from a galvanized lamp, a gas lamp, hanging from the center of the concrete ceiling. William walked closer toward the light and chair. There is a child bound, a boy. Lashed by a braided rope, not by reverse ply bindings, but braids. The boy is wounded, but not his neck: the left side of his chest is bleeding and dry. The boy is unconscious. William squinted his eyes and rolled them slowly to the left and the right sensing something, like a ghost. William unbraided the rope whips dangling from the chair's arms and lifted the boy up—holding him to his chest like a mother holding an infant.

The boy began to wake. William walked back to the steps of the bar, for some reason he felt safe there, and laid the boy down on the boardwalk, William unshouldered his pack and used it to lay the boys head. He inspected the wound on the boy's chest. There is an X cut deeply into his flesh. The wound is still bleeding. The boy is coming too.

"Who did this to you? What happened? Why are you here? Who are you?"

The boy began to scream and shake and cry and mumble. William grabbed ahold of him and pulled him softly and tight to his chest. The boy's eyes opened, and he saw William's face, they both passed out, and while this happened the bank and bricks and the bars fell to the ground, silently.

The sound of glass shaking, vibrating, and shattering wakes them up, in unison. With a gasp the boy answered, "Nemo! Nemo did this to me. He wants my heart. He tried to cut it out. He was about to pull my ribs apart and take it. I felt the knife grinding on my chest since the day I was brought here. I didn't know if you'd come in time. While I was awake the pain subsided. And when I passed out I had nightmares of children slain and dead: they were walking in the streets, everywhere, wandering with arteries pumping something unreal, wandering without a heart." *wandering without wonder . . .*

"Boy, is this real? Is this place real or a dream."

"This is real. William, where is Israel?"

"How do you know my name? How do you know Izzy? Kid. Who are you?"

"I don't know . . . exactly . . . how I know you. I only knew that the only way I wouldn't end up like the other kids was if the two of you found me in time. Where is Izzy?"

"I've been tracking him through the desert. I think he went into the mountains."

"William. My chest. I'm afraid to look."

William reached behind the boy's head where the pack was and pulled out Izzy's small pouch. Inside he found some iodine, a bandana, and some hundred-mile tape. The cut was a clean-cut gaping wide open, which made it easy to sterilize. William gave the boy a folded bandana to bite down on, then began pouring the iodine into the fleshy grooves. William reached for the tape and tore off two pieces. The boy's wound looked like four triangles of flesh separated by bloody canyons of muscle. The bones showed through a little. William thought of it as bedrock: strong tough stone. William used the tape as a sort of butterfly bandage taping one triangle of flesh toward the other, bringing to disconnected parts of body together again, he did this with both sets of triangles. Now, he has two X's on his chest . . . one that wants to pull apart and one that wants to pull together—tension and compression, together.

William couldn't help but wonder why any creature would reach for a heart through the rib cage when tearing though his guts and punching through the diaphragm would be much easier—like any other wild creature would. It seems that Nemo was not quite a creature and not quite a man. *What were Nemo's plans with the boy? Was his plan to take the boy's heart? Or, was his plan more sinister? What was he going to do after reaching the heart? Take it? If the children from this boy's dream were still pumping something in their arteries surely there hearts were still inside—maybe—just different.* Or, were they replaced with something new?

William's thoughts trailed off from his thinking of how and why and who, into where. Him and this boy are here *alone* in the desert. The boy is strong, he is still alive.

The key in the door fell to the ground and slowly rolled down the steps into the sand and became a gun once again. The gun has changed somehow: changed in a slight way, so slight that William did not notice. It's only a scratch in the brass—but a mark was made and a mark remains filed into the memory of the gun. Filed in time. Night becomes day.

How many days have passed in this town? It seems like one of three or three of one. William is unsure. The sun is on its second rise, or is it the third? But something about that doesn't set well in William's mind. He felt as though eternity had passed by in a mere blink of on eye; and yet, so many things have transpired, transcribed, and . . . well, the intensity of events just seem strange, events that led from one to the next started, it seems, with the spinning of a revolver; a gun that transformed, somehow.

Long ago a king pulled a gun from a fire burning in the sky to share with his queen for all eternity. The queen soon came with a gift of her own she had pulled from a hole in the night. As their gifts became one their thoughts became many, scattered through space and time. It was the moment of marriage that shattered their ties into fragments of glass in sand; a gun fired once with passion and love fell into another queen's hands; awaiting the day of love's true face she holds the gun at her hip, knowing full well the gun will not fire until returned to its place of desire.

Interverbum

I must warn you, dear reader, if you continue on, some of the mystery will be lost—but not all. Ahead I've decided to write about some of the symbols, some of the depths behind the layer of adventure you've already traveled. I'm sure you've caught on to some, maybe all, of what I've written; even though this will not be all-inclusive, it may shed some light. I must confess, dear reader, not even I fully understand all the words I write—as the story is still being written.

If you wish to leave with the mystery and wait for the following parts to come—wait for part two and stop now. Otherwise, turn the page . . .

Jacob Burnard

So you've decided to turn the page, good. I have another confession . . . While, reading the following will shed light—it may also cast a shadow; in truth, one cannot exist without the other—nothing will.

Jacob Burnard

I Live for Her Tears

Eli's Kindness Ring The Eagle Will

By Walter I. Calman

This book is dedicated to the inquisitive reader—the inquisitive mind. I hope you find the turns and bends that lead to many ends—finding our soul in the process.

The Title

    I've taken great pains to shroud the mystery within layer upon layer. Like a child who has mined for gold deep below the earth who has then returned to his mineshaft as a man to find his mine caved in with rocks and rubble that he has never seen. We will see unfold some of the layers placed in his path.

    Killing Angels in The Wilderness, is an anagram: *Eli's Kindness Ring the Eagle Will.* Undoubtedly these may ring a bell in your mind concerning religious stories, as they should. Many of us, when we were young grew up hearing the stories in the Old Testament Bible. Abraham, a man of great faith or insanity, begot Isaac, whom he almost killed as a sacrifice as the voice of god had commanded. Interestingly, God was only testing Abraham's faith and Isaac was safe. Isaac begot Jacob and Esau. Jacob was a bit of a trickster. Jacob, as the younger, fooled his blind father into believing he was Esau—he wanted birthright. Why? Envy? Jealousy? Power? Perhaps the voice of god directed him to do so. The important matter is that Jacob succeeded. And succeeding would be the trend for Jacob. Though he faced great adversity, Jacob paved his way and later became Israel.

    Eli came later, the meaning of Eli is accent, and he also became blind toward the end of his days and died at the ripe old age of 98. Some say Eli was too kind. He did not rebuke his sons' wicked ways. By wicked they were acting on the id, out of balance with the other aspects of mind and soul—without a gyroscope.

The subtitle also includes four anagrams for four lines of a riddle, an easy rhyme, *I Live for Her Tears,* is one of them. The others will be reveled in parts Two, Three, and Four. Back to the main title . . . There are twenty-eight letters in the title. Twenty-eight so happens to be a perfect number. A perfect number is a number that is half the sum of all of its positive divisors. Euclid dubbed these numbers perfect, ideal, or complete numbers, depending on how you translate Greek. Though, why even bother with perfect numbers? What's the big deal? Let's combine some religious ideas with mathematics and physics, why not? The first perfect number is six; according to the Old Testament Bible, God created Man on the sixth day. This is significant to William and Izzy's story because we are following them on a journey of the trials and tests many young men face—temptation being the first. The second perfect number is twenty-eight. The Moon's orbit and its phases average approximately twenty-eight days, fascinating. We could go on down the number hole for days; but I'm no mathematician. What is important to know is that those principles foreshadow the realization of balance in the minds of William and Izzy, internal and external.

The Highway

On Highway Nine, or is it six? we learn a little bit about Izzy. He is a thinker, he wants to understand things, and through playing strategic games he hopes to reveal thoughts in other peoples' minds. He thinks that others look at these games as challenges to take on—a competition.

Izzy sees it as a way to look into peoples' minds and souls without having to look in their eyes—without them knowing what he is up to. Izzy doesn't mind losing the game; because, even in doing so he is winning information, he is gaining knowledge. Sometimes he acts shy to size other people up. Sometimes he will speak bluntly for the same reason. Izzy never uses these tricks on William, though. He trusts William even though he doesn't fully understand him—William has never steered Izzy wrong.

Izzy also has a deep secret—he wants to fall in love. He hopes that by some chance he will meet the girl of his dreams—a girl that will be the gleam in his eyes until the day he dies, or longer—a girl from the moon, a girl that will jump over the moon to find him, as he will jump over the Sun to find her—"The Wind Cries Mary" but Izzy only sees a princess. One he can rescue. One to rescue him.

One to end loneliness for them both. The plight of the human mind and the savior of humankind—thirsty for a mate of body and mind. My soul drowned in a tavern, lost in a cavern and up in the clouds. My soul is thirsty, yes. My soul is on fire.

Okay, more numbers . . .Physics . . . 108 is mentioned in the rhyme about the tires rolling and treading, tearing and tearing . . . tearing up in my eyes and tearing away the surprise. Interestingly the distance from the Moon to the Earth is 108 times the Moon's diameter. Also, The distance from the Sun to the Earth is 108 times the Sun's diameter. This is a meaningful coincidence. Though, both the Earth's and the Moon's orbits are elliptical so these figures are not constant. There's even more to this number: 108 is also significant in some religions. And, not so significant is also the number of cards in a deck of UNO tee-em. One Zero Eight, the Moon away . . . the Sun, too.

Betsy the bus, like a train, is taking them away from their place of comfort to a destination unknown, all things play their part. This name was chosen for its association with the names of famous people and fictional vehicles: In Arthur C. Clark's, *2001: A Space Odyssey*, A vehicle called The Moonbus was used to transport people over the surface of the moon; and, the EVA that HAL 9000 used to murder Frank Poole was named betty; Bessie is the name of the yellow roadster from *Doctor Who*. Also, Bess is Harry Houdini's wife. Betsy the bus is a vehicle with these similar and familiar attributes: she brings us to the desert of memories, she takes us to the surface of the Moon, she carries us to the far reaches of space, she is faithful, she has her tricks, she is grounded.

There is always water in the air. The fire brings it there. The earth keeps it there. The wind sends it to rivers. The rivers flow to the shallows of the caves and Bythos of the ocean. From the depths of the sea there springs a twin beyond time reflecting light toward the sky for the heavens to see two brothers bring Sophia to me that we may be more than a virtue to men and a man more than a thought to she. More than a knight in shining amour dropped from the sky as a god to worship. More than a floating dream lost to fantasy. More than a home built from stone and bone. More than a blaze of passion sent back to the air. More than the eclipse of the sun and the moon—inversum. More than the light of a ship passing in the night. More than the constant cyclical that does not exist. More than all of these are the elliptical interplays of the divine.

William and Izzy hear the coyote's cries in the moonless night; tearing apart a mother's kind foreshadows the disgust to come, not in this book but the next, of terror and torcher. Here, William will come to another fork in the road toward Izzy. A child, a little girl—trapped in the current, stuck in the red clay of the past, sinking in the sand . . .

The House

The Way Station Izzy does not want to see brings him to dreams and realities of great emotion.

Remembering is painful and the creation of new memories is sure to bring more heartache. Izzy wants to keep these parts hidden from himself, he has run and done this well. Izzy has come to trust William over the years. He has come to trust William's prodding and brooding over his thoughts and dreams and doings—but he is not ready. He has not been trained to tackle himself and his fears . . . though, he has been taught the principles of survival, and he knows, as much as it scares him, some things are best met head-on . . . The waves of deep seas can break on stern and starboard; but are better met at bow.

Through training from his father, Izzy has always had contingencies based on the probability of events—like a game of chess. But sometimes he just forgets. And, as he remembers those things he forgot, such as water, he adapts. Izzy knows other forces exist; He is not blind to faith but sometimes his eyes are not open—this is when the true magic happens—he has faith that his dreams will unlock those memories in the myriad of stars just over the horizon—of pyramids and Orion. He has faith, yet he is often afraid of the unknown and forgotten places; the forgotten faces of his past. It is much easier to peer into the soul of another . . . it is another matter when one knows they must peer into their own soul . . . when one must peer into the spinning, whirling, turning of events already had, the places at hand, and the future he has and dreams one wishes to plan.

A gyroscope spins and wobbles its pole, like the Earth at its North, to balance those things it holds—holding it. Staring and studying its movements in relation to what surrounds it. Will surrounds the balancing gadget and is fascinated by its hypnotic movements. While Izzy is obsessed with water: with a well and a wish, with a want for the pit to ascend into memory and understand his true purpose—to know what that is. By breaking the lock on the hidden water and drinking the memories from within the ground, he sees something there, something special and profound—something worth wishing for. For his special task has whisked him into the air and set his mind to fire, to leave William to his own devises, and to free himself unto unseen places that hold a specific destination. A destination he will see without the aid of a cartographer's mind or a map to read—flying only on the wings of faith. What did Izzy wish for as he placed the amazonite pendant on the well? Love? A girl? A queen? Mary?

Amazonite is an important sigil. It has shades of turquois and greens like the ancient waters buried deep below earth. It is called the stone of courage and truth, empowering the bearer to discover truths and integrities from within. Amazonite provides balance of the mind. Amazonite also shares its name with the Amazon warriors of

Greek legend—women warriors—women who fought and died alongside men, Woman covered with the tattoos from their dreams and life and geometry, women who loved deeply. The Greeks of old villainized these heroic woman warriors and created disturbing stories and myth that some still believe true today; but a diligent researcher will cull the lies and discover their truths.

There is truth in Izzy's dream and this is one he doesn't want to remember. He does not want to share this with William; he knows William cares and will help bring hidden things into light. Many lights cast shadows, Izzy knows, and does not want to face those, even though he knows it's going to happen—he knows . . . it must happen. Izzy knows the book his mother brought to his dream is a book of life—Izzy's book of life, full of blank pages, he must continue to write. Fate does not decide what is wrought in those pages, though fate does support the life he has chosen—and that night, through the water and the well and the tears they cried, Izzy chose to mine and to build the river of his mind. Israel chose to wrestle with God.

Jacob Burnard

The Town

    William is alone with inuit eyes left to focus solely on the surprise—Izzy is gone . . . left his pride and possessions in the mud for William to find.

    Blade and book and bone; chain and lock and stone. William is headed on the journey Izzy knows he too is traveling—they travel together—always. Izzy is faith, William is will—together they endure. Together, and alone, they pace down The River of Israel. Together they carry on through different paths that hold the same mission . . . a mission toward . . .

    The Sonoran Queen, the minstrel, the muse, the siren, the lady of anguish—all are different and all the same. William has wandered toward her beauty, toward her trap and she will capture him. She is in pain for the love she has not gained, all the faces are the same but she continues to play the game—to win a prize—to win William's eyes, to hold his face so he will take the place of the forgotten faces. Regina, alone, will never win. There is only one end to her story and that is death. But death is not the end for her; she is now a constant memory and reminder in William's head. And she will always be with him. His thoughts will always wander toward her and his heart will always know what has been done—what must be done if the Sonoran Queen returns in some other form. He has her gun holstered on his left side to reminisce and recall the strength of mind and the assuring voice inside beckoning him to be *Vilhelmus Filius Vis*. To be what he has always been.

Purely by coincidence The Sonoran Queen also seems to be the, "Cowgirl in The Sand" written by Neil Young. I have not found an interpretation of this song that rings anywhere near what it means to me, but great art follows many eyes to see the scene however they please . . . this is what I see, "Cowgirl in The Sand" shows the perceptions of a man observing the possible dimensions of a woman in play. In the first stanza she is The Cowgirl in The Sand and in command of his passions. Then he sees she is a siren. Her name changes to Ruby in The Dust and might just be a lady he can trust but the band she had around him has begun to rust and he breaks free to see she is The Queen of his dreams. Purple words are royalty and grey background is periphery in nighttime light. And, although he has loved her, and still does—he lets her go from sand to dust to dreams because She is not complete and He cannot let go of the dream.

Two waters diverge in the desert sand, one in wind and one in land. They cross and pass overhead and under tests in a land of life and death bound by shackles of sacred contracts to a life chosen from beyond time imbedded in a temporal mind trying to find the figures in their minds bending light on a path to understand what is real and what is sand to bend the band and break free the other shackles that beckon me. She was here and now she's dead and lies awake on distant shores. Calling me. Drawing me in her soul the battered man who's washed ashore.

Click-clack, click-clack . . .tick-tock, tick-tock . . .The clock is cocked. The slide unlocked. Sulfur and stardust fill the air and waft sweet honey perfume through our hair.

Jacob Burnard

Afterword

Dear faithful reader, your name has changed. You've braved the nave and continued on. You are faith, and I've been here, waiting for you at the end of Part One to greet you yet again and to warn you—the writers and cast of this story are many and all have been caste in shadow and light. I have just one more question for you before you put me away—who did you hear speaking after interverbum? . . . The narrator . . . The author . . . Was it me? Or . . . some other clever creature . . .

Readers' Notes

I've left this place bare for your thoughts, for your poems, for love.

Readers' Notes

Readers' Notes

Readers' Notes

Readers' Notes

ABOUT THE AUTHOR

Jake . . . that's how he's known, and that's what I call him. With the exception of an occasional *Mountain Man* or *Grizzly Adams* reference due to his beard and big boned features, that's what everybody calls him. . . Jake. Born in southern California in 1982, he was the youngest with two tough brothers and a passionately assertive sister. Not a privileged or a formally educated family, but that gave Jake what really mattered – the ability and essentially an open-ended invitation to be whatever he desired.

His mother was taken by cancer in the year 2000 at the young age of 44. Jake was only seventeen. The world was wide open . . . *an open book*. Although tragic, this gave Jake the opportunity to become his own, to forge his own way down the prickly and elliptical path we all call *life*.

In order to provide for his beautiful little daughter and himself in Menifee, California, Jake has used his large stature and strength to earn a living working outdoors in the construction business. In addition to having a big heart and loving family, Jake has always loved nature. Nature. . . It only makes sense that he went to school and studied environmental and behavioral science.

Jake's love of nature and people has inspired him to create adventures such as his annual barefoot hike through the Cleveland

National Forest. Not to mention, his signature ranch festivities where ax-throwing and wood chopping were always a fun and friendly competition among those close to him. These are just a few of his exciting escapades!

More importantly, Jake's love of nature and family has remained paramount and inspired him to write. Following his heart, Jake takes artistry to a whole "'nother" level. His different and uniquely abstract, but surprisingly understanding writings touch a vein in the artery of his readers that inspire adventures and offers lessons for everyone. His life experiences and artistic imagination have inspired the creation of this trilogy that I am sure will arouse the passion of countless readers for long into the future.

~Daniel L. Vinson

www.ingramcontent.com/pod-product-compliance
Lightning Source LLC
Chambersburg PA
CBHW062130160426
43191CB00013B/2259